Our Skeleton

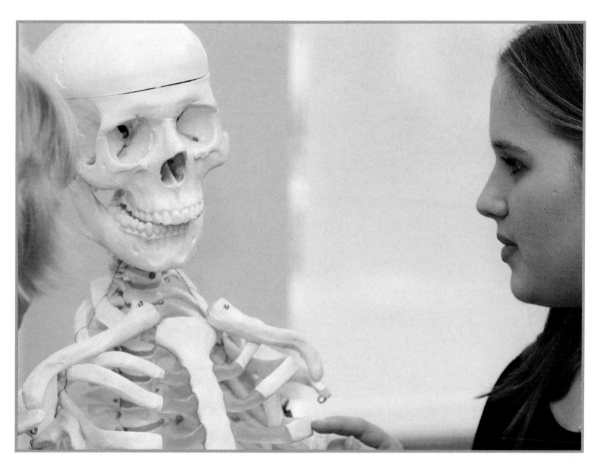

Susan Thames

Rourke
Publishing LLC
Vero Beach, Florida 32964

www.rourkepublishing.com

PHOTO CREDITS: © Timothy Babasade: title page; © Renee Brady: pages 4, 5, 7, 9, 11, 17, 21, 22; © Linda Bucklin: page 13; © Bonnie Jacobs: page 15; © Josef Philipp: page 19.

Editor: Robert Stengard-Olliges

Cover design by Michelle Moore.

Library of Congress Cataloging-in-Publication Data

Thames, Susan.
  Our skeleton / Susan Thames.
     p. cm. -- (Our bodies)
  Includes bibliographical references and index.
  ISBN 978-1-60044-514-9 (Hardcover)
  ISBN 978-1-60044-675-7 (Softcover)
  1. Skeleton--Juvenile literature. 2. Bones--Juvenile literature. I. Title.
  QM101.T43 2008
  611'.71--dc22
                                2007011849

Printed in the USA

CG/CG

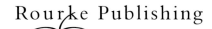

Rourke Publishing

www.rourkepublishing.com – rourke@rourkepublishing.com
Post Office Box 3328, Vero Beach, FL 32964

Table of Contents

Bones, Bones, Bones

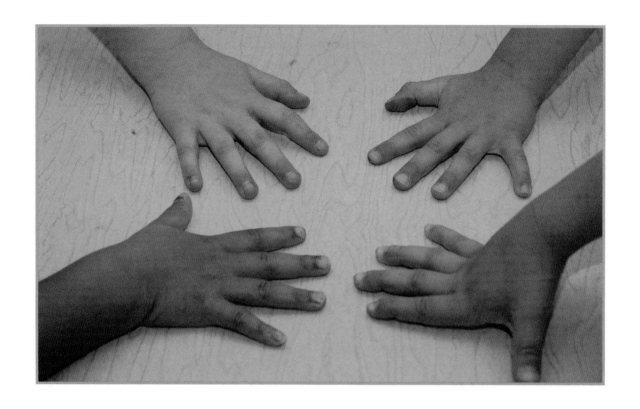

Look at your hands.

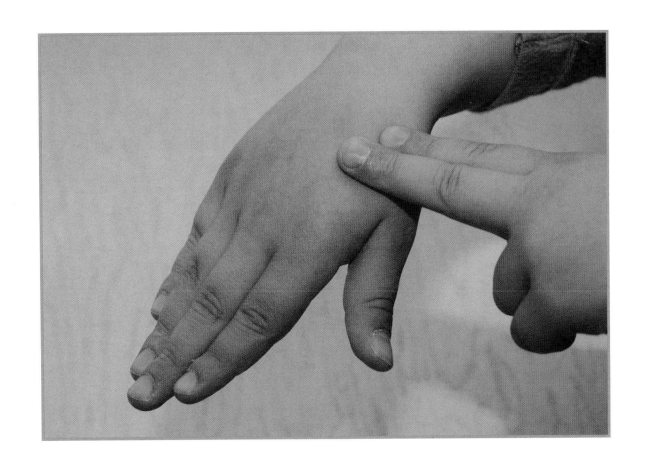

Feel the bones in your hands.

Bones are all shapes
and sizes.

The biggest bone is in your leg.

9

The smallest bone is inside your ear.

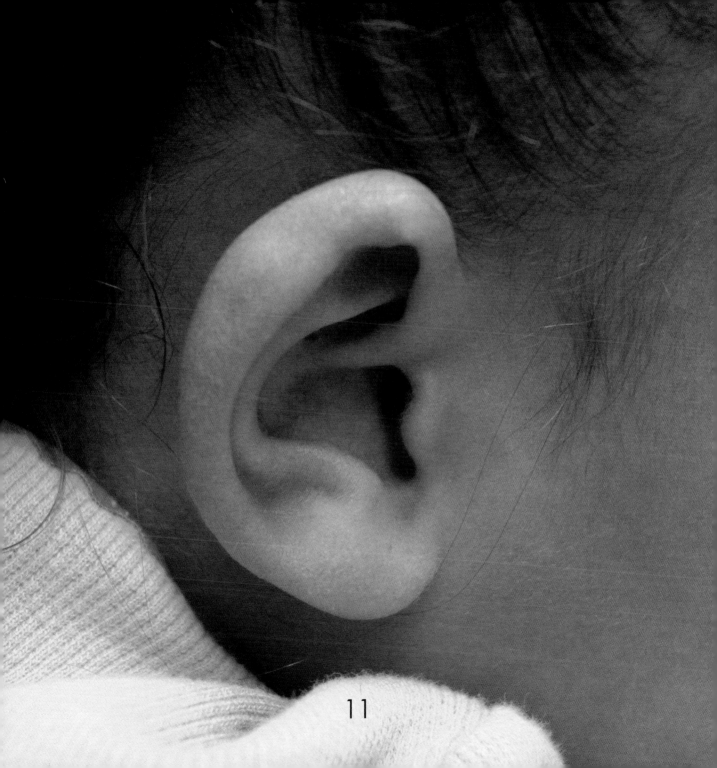

11

Your Skeleton

Your **skeleton** has 206 bones.

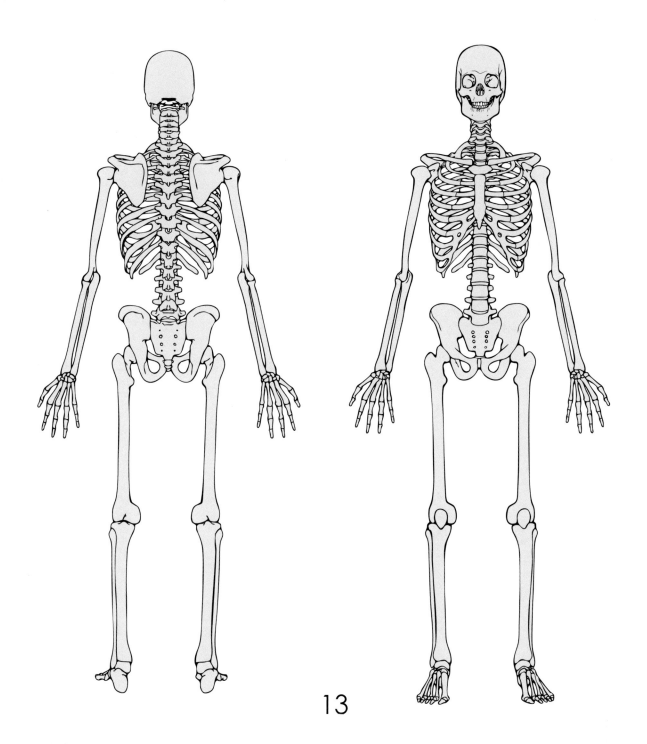

13

Your skeleton holds you up.

Your skeleton helps you move.

Your skeleton **protects** your **organs**.

Healthy Bones

Milk is good for your bones.

Exercise is good for your bones.

Glossary

exercise (EK sur size) — to move your body in a way that makes you strong and healthy

organs (OR guhnz) — soft parts of your body that work to keep you alive

protects (pruh TEKTZ) — keep safe

skeleton (SKEL uh tuhn) — all the bones in your body

Index

Further Reading

Arnold, Caroline. *The Skeletal System*. Lerner
  Publications Company, 2005.
Lindeen, Carol. *My Bones*. Pebble Books, 2007.

Websites to Visit

www.kidshealth.org
www.healthfinder.gov/kids
www.yucky.discovery.com

About the Author

Susan Thames, a former elementary school teacher, lives in Tampa, Florida. She enjoys spending time with her grandsons and hopes to instill in them a love of reading and a passion for travel.